To my two boys, this book is for you.
I wish you happiness.

Stay in touch at www.piccopuppy.com and @PiccoPuppy on Instagram and Facebook.

I Wish You Happiness is available in personalized, bilingual, French, Spanish, Italian, German, Chinese, and Japanese editions. Visit www.piccopuppy.com for more information.

A special thanks to my wonderful team: Ann Baratashvili (illustrator), David Miles (book designer), Alina Zhang (printer), and Anna Wang (printer).

Font Credits
Lost Brush by Stripes Studio
Marck Script by Denis Masharov
Cormorant Upright by Christian Thalmann
Century Schoolbook by Morris Fuller Benton
Copse by Dan Rhatigan
Josefin Sans by Santiago Orozco

First published in 2020 by Picco Puppy
Reprinted in 2023

Marketing Munch Pty Limited DBA Picco Puppy, PO Box 103, Killara, NSW 2071, Australia
Picco Puppy® is a registered trademark of Marketing Munch Pty Limited

A catalog record for this book is available from the National Library of Australia
ISBN 978-1-925973-12-9

Printed and bound in China

I Wish You Happiness

MICHAEL WONG · ANN BARATASHVILI

I wish you *dreams* and
aspirations, to spread
your wings and reach
for the stars.

I wish you *courage* and *strength*, for the magic begins at the end of your comfort zone.

I wish you *imagination* and *creativity*, for the world is a blank canvas to paint your masterpiece.

I wish you *adventure* and *curiosity*, to go where there is no path and leave a trail.

I wish you *health* and *well-being*, for they are worth more than all the riches in the world.

I wish you *peace* and **tranquility**, to listen to the birds and gaze at the stars.

I wish you *knowledge*
and *wisdom*, for they
are the foundations of a
successful life.

I wish you *grit* and *resilience*, to never ever give up.

I wish you *success*
and *prosperity*, to
trust yourself and your
ability to succeed.

I wish you *luck* and *opportunity*, for the more you try, the luckier you get.

I wish you *faith* and *hope*, to believe everything will be all right.

I wish you *family* and *friendships*, for they are life's greatest sources of happiness.

I wish you *joy* and *laughter*, to laugh long and loud until you gasp for breath.

I wish you *kindness* and *generosity*, for no act of kindness is ever wasted, no matter how small.

I wish you *love* and *affection*, to fill your beautiful heart with an ocean of joy.

I wish you all those wonderful things,
but most of all . . .

I wish you
happiness!

Can You Spot the Famous People?

No matter what obstacles you face, believe in yourself and all that you are—
just like these famous people did. Can you spot all five in the book?

Can you spot a young Neil Armstrong?

Neil Armstrong was a famous astronaut. He was the first person
to walk on the moon in 1969. Before that, he was an experimental
research test pilot, which is a very dangerous job.

Can you spot a young Katherine Johnson?

Katherine Johnson was a mathematician. Her calculations helped
send the Apollo 11 rocket, carrying Neil Armstrong and his fellow
astronauts, to the moon.

Can you spot a young Amelia Earhart?

Amelia Earhart was the first female aviator to fly solo across
the Atlantic Ocean. She helped to create "The Ninety-Nines," an
international organization of women pilots.

Can you spot a young J. K. Rowling?

Twelve publishers rejected J. K. Rowling's first book. She had to wait a
year before her book was finally published. Her "Harry Potter" books
went on to become the best-selling book series in history.

Can you spot a young Alexander Selkirk?

Alexander Selkirk spent four years as a castaway on an uninhabited
island. His survival story inspired Daniel Defoe's "Robinson Crusoe."
It is often credited as the first English novel, published in 1719.

Can You Spot the Dogs?

There are seventeen dogs and one cat in the book. Can you spot them all?

Beagle

Cavalier King
Charles Spaniel

Dalmatian

French Bulldog

German
Shepherd

Golden
Retriever

Jack Russell
Terrier

Labrador
Retriever

Maltese

Pomeranian

Poodle

Pug

Saint Bernard

Shiba Inu

Siamese Cat

Welsh Corgi

West Highland
Terrier

Yorkshire
Terrier

Hi, it's Michael here. I hope you enjoyed the book.
Did you know there are more books in
"The Unconditional Love Series"?
I hope you collect them all.

As an appreciation for your kind support,
claim your gift at www.piccopuppy.com/gift.

Michael Wong is an award-winning children's author. He is passionate about creating beautiful, empowering, diverse, and inclusive books for children. Michael lives with his wife and two children in Sydney, Australia.

Ann Baratashvili is an award-winning illustrator and concept artist. She won first prize in the 2009 DeviantArt/ Wacom "Bring Your Vision to Life: Dreams" contest. Ann lives with her husband and son in Tbilisi, Georgia.

The Unconditional Love Series

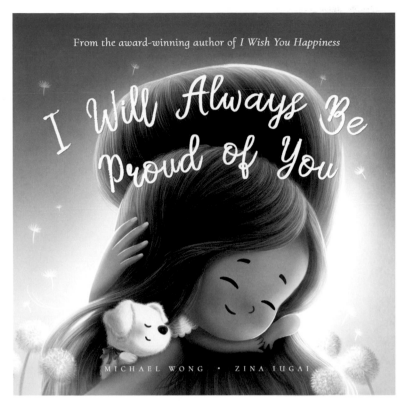

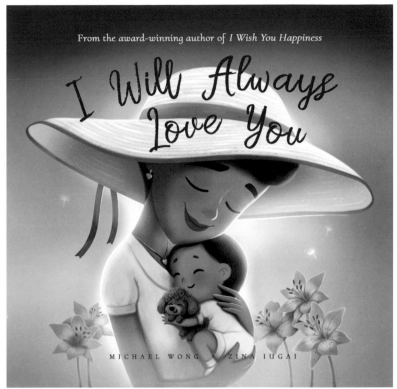

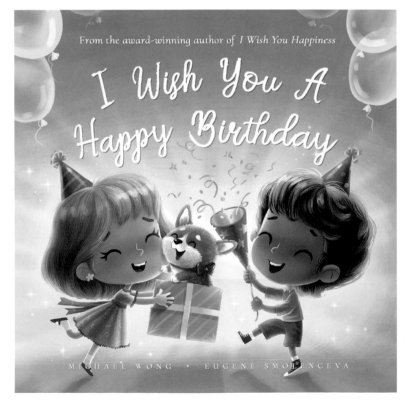

Available at all good bookstores
and PiccoPuppy.com.